MOMENTS OF TRUTH

VOLUME TWO

MOMENTS OF TRUTH

VOLUME TWO

Excerpts from
Autobiography of a Yogi
by Paramhansa Yogananda

Reprint of the Philosophical Library
1946 First Edition

Crystal Clarity, Publishers
Nevada City, California

Hardbound edition, first printing 1997

Compilation copyright © Crystal Clarity, Publishers

Original photographs by J. Donald Walters
Original cover art by Sara Brink
Cover art and illustrations by Christine Starner Schuppe

Quotations from **Autobiography of a Yogi**
Selected by Mel Bly

Printed in China

Crystal Clarity, Publishers
14618 Tyler-Foote Road
Nevada City, California 95959

1-800-424-1055
Website: http://www.consciousnet.com/CrystalClarity

Introduction

This book contains timeless wisdom for meeting life's challenges. These excerpts from **Autobiography of a Yogi** are words to live by: insights from one of the great mystics of our time. People often don't grasp the depth of the teachings in the **Autobiography of a Yogi**, so in pulling out gems from the book, one can perceive these truths more easily. Followers of many religious traditions have come to recognize **Autobiography of a Yogi** as a masterpiece of spiritual literature. Paramhansa Yogananda was the first yoga master of India whose mission it was to live and teach in the West. **Autobiography of a Yogi** contains Yogananda's first-hand account of visits to saints and masters of India, the years of training he received in the ashram of his guru, and long-secret teachings of Self-realization.

—J. Donald Walters

God is simple.
Everything else
is complex.

Chapter Five
Page Forty-Two

Man can understand
no eternal verity
until he has
freed himself
from pretensions.

Chapter Five
Page Forty-Three

Struggles of the battlefields
pale into insignificance
when man first contends
with inward enemies!

Chapter Five
Page Forty-Three

Bricks and mortar
sing us no audible tune;
the heart opens
only to the human
chant of being.

Chapter Five
Page Forty-Four

Ordinary love is selfish,
darkly rooted in desires
and satisfactions.
Divine love is
without condition,
without boundary,
without change.

Chapter Ten
Page Ninety-One

Attachment is blinding;
it lends an
imaginary halo
of attractiveness
to the object of desire.

Chapter Twelve
Page One Hundred Five

It is not the
physical scientist
but the fully
self-realized master
who comprehends
the true nature
of matter.

Chapter Twelve
Page One Hundred Fifteen

Imagination is
the door
through which
disease as well as
healing enters.

Chapter Twelve
Page One Hundred Twenty

Good manners
without sincerity
are like a beautiful
dead lady.

Chapter Twelve
Page One Hundred Twenty-One

The hard core
of human egotism
is hardly to be dislodged
except rudely.
With its departure,
the Divine finds at last
an unobstructed channel.

Chapter Twelve
Page One Hundred Twenty-Two

A saint's courage
roots in his
compassion for
the stumbling eyeless
of this world.

Chapter Twelve
Page One Hundred Twenty-Four

Keen intelligence
is two-edged.
It may be used
constructively
or destructively
like a knife,
either to cut
the boil of ignorance,
or to decapitate one's self.

Just as a man,
impersonating a woman,
does not become one,
so the soul,
impersonating
both man and woman,
has no sex.
The soul is the pure,
changeless image of God.

Chapter Twelve
Page One Hundred Twenty-Seven

Small yearnings
are openings
in the reservoir
of your inner peace,
permitting healing waters
to be wasted
in the desert soil
of materialism.

Chapter Twelve
Page One Hundred Twenty-Eight

Finding God
will mean
the funeral
of all sorrows.

Chapter Twelve
Page One Hundred Twenty-Nine

Do not confuse
understanding
with a
larger vocabulary.

Chapter Twelve
Page One Hundred Thirty-One

Softer than the flower,
where kindness
is concerned;
stronger than
the thunder,
where principles
are at stake.

Chapter Twelve
Page One Hundred Thirty-Three

Some people
try to be tall by
cutting off the
heads of others!

Chapter Twelve
Page One Hundred Thirty-Four

What one does not
trouble to find within
will not be discovered
by transporting
the body
hither and yon.

Chapter Thirteen,
Page One Hundred Thirty-Eight

A master bestows
the divine experience
of cosmic consciousness
when his disciple,
by meditation,
has strengthened his mind
to a degree where the
vast vistas would not
overwhelm him.

Chapter Fourteen
Page One Hundred Forty-Six

Spiritual advancement
is not measured by
one's outward powers,
but only by the depth
of his bliss
in meditation.

Chapter Fourteen
Page One Hundred Forty-Eight

Outward longings
drive us from
the Eden within;
they offer
false pleasures
which only impersonate
soul-happiness.

Chapter Fourteen
Page One Hundred Forty-Eight

As the power
of a radio
depends on the amount
of electrical current
it can utilize,
so the human radio
is energized according to
the power of will
possessed by
each individual.

Chapter Fifteen
Page One Hundred Fifty-Four

The truths—
those surprising,
amazing, unforeseen
truths—which
our descendants
will discover,
are even now
all around us,
staring us in the eyes,
and yet we
do not see them.

Chapter Fifteen
Page One Hundred Fifty-Five

The soul is
ever-free;
it is deathless
because birthless.

Chapter Sixteen
Page One Hundred Sixty-Three

Seeds of
past karma
cannot germinate
if they are roasted
in the divine fires
of wisdom.

Chapter Sixteen
Page One Hundred Sixty-Six

The deeper the
self-realization
of a man,
the more he influences
the whole universe
by his subtle
spiritual vibrations.

Chapter Sixteen
Page One Hundred Sixty-Seven

The first duty of man
is to keep his body
in good condition;
otherwise his mind
is unable
to remain fixed
in devotional
concentration.

Chapter Twenty-One
Page Two Hundred

A sickly body
does not indicate
that a guru is not
in touch with
divine powers,
any more than
lifelong health
necessarily indicates
an inner illumination.

Chapter Twenty-One
Page Two Hundred One

Spiritual sight,
x-raylike,
penetrates into all matter;
the divine eye is
center everywhere,
circumference nowhere.

Chapter Twenty-Two
Page Two Hundred Five

A true yogi may
remain dutifully
in the world;
there he is like
butter on water,
and not like the
easily-diluted milk
of unchurned and
undisciplined humanity.

Chapter Twenty-Four
Page Two Hundred Twenty-Two

Yoga combines
the bodily
and the spiritual
with each other
in an extraordinarily
complete way.

Chapter Twenty-Four
Page Two Hundred Twenty Three

The Western day
is indeed nearing
when the inner science
of self-control
will be found
as necessary as
the outer conquest
of nature.

Chapter Twenty-Four
Page Two Hundred Twenty Four

Neutralizing
decay and growth,
by quieting the heart,
the yogi learns
life control.

Chapter Twenty-Six
Page Two Hundred Thirty-Two

One-half minute
of revolution of energy
around the sensitive
spinal cord of man
effects subtle progress
in his evolution;
that half-minute of *Kriya*
equals one year
of natural spiritual
unfoldment.

Chapter Twenty-Six
Page Two Hundred Thirty-Four

Man requires
a million years
of normal
diseaseless evolution
to perfect his
human brain
sufficiently to express
cosmic consciousness.

Chapter Twenty-Six
Page Two Hundred Thirty-Four

The ancient
yogic technique
converts the breath
into mind.
By spiritual advancement,
one is able to
cognize the breath
as an act of mind—
a dream-breath.

Chapter Twenty-Six
Page Two Hundred Thirty-Five

The yoga method
overcomes the
tug of war
between the mind
and the
matter-bound senses,
and frees the devotee
to reinherit
his eternal kingdom.

Chapter Twenty-Six
Page Two Hundred Thirty-Six

The superior method
of soul living
frees the yogi who,
shorn of his ego-prison,
tastes the deep air
of omnipresence.

Chapter Twenty-Six
Page Two Hundred Thirty-Seven

Each man's
intellectual reactions,
feelings, moods,
and habits
are circumscribed
by effects of past causes,
whether of this
or a prior life.

Chapter Twenty-Six
Page Two Hundred Thirty-Eight

The burden of the years
has no ill effect
on a great yogi's
full possession
of supreme
spiritual powers.

Chapter Twenty-Seven
Page Two Hundred Forty-Seven

He who knows
himself as the
omnipresent Spirit
is subject no longer
to the rigidities
of a body in
time and space.

Chapter Thirty
Page Two Hundred Sixty-Six

The tragedy of death
is unreal;
those who shudder at it
are like an ignorant actor
who dies of fright
on the stage
when nothing more
is fired at him
than a blank cartridge.

Chapter Thirty
Page Two Hundred Seventy

One's values are
profoundly changed
when he is
finally convinced
that creation is only
a vast motion picture,
and that not in it,
but beyond it,
lies his own reality.

Chapter Thirty
Page Two Hundred Seventy

A humanity
at peace
will know the
endless fruits of victory,
sweeter to the taste
than any nurtured
on the soil of blood.

Chapter Thirty-Two
Page Two Hundred Eighty-Six

Toward realization
of the world's
highest ideal—peace
through brotherhood—
may yoga, the science
of personal contact
with the Divine,
spread in time
to all men in all lands.

Chapter Thirty-Two
Page Two Hundred Eighty-Six

A man closes his eyes
and erects a dream-creation which, on
awakening,
he effortlessly
dematerializes.
Similarly,
when he awakens
in cosmic consciousness,
he will effortlessly
dematerialize the illusions
of the cosmic dream.

Chapter Thirty-Four
Page Three Hundred Three

The karmic law
requires that
every human wish
find ultimate fulfillment.
Desire is thus the chain
which binds man
to the reincarnational wheel.

Chapter Thirty-Four
Page Three Hundred Two

A common stone
locks within itself
the secret of stupendous
atomic energy;
even so, a mortal
is yet a powerhouse
of divinity.

Chapter Thirty Four
Page Three Hundred Four

Meditate unceasingly,
that you may quickly
behold yourself
as the Infinite Essence,
free from every
form of misery.
Cease being a prisoner
of the body;
using the secret
key of Kriya,
learn to escape into Spirit.

Chapter Thirty-Five
Page Three Hundred Fifteen

Our eagerness
for worldly activity
kills in us
the sense of
spiritual awe.

Chapter Thirty-Five
Page Three Hundred Twenty-One

Destroy all the sacred
books on yoga,
its fundamental laws
will come out
whenever there appears
a true yogi who
comprises within himself
pure devotion
and consequently
pure knowledge.

Chapter Thirty-Five
Page Three Hundred Twenty-Two

Divine union is possible
through self-effort,
and is not dependent
on theological beliefs
or on the arbitrary will
of a Cosmic Dictator.

Chapter Thirty-Five
Page Three Hundred Twenty-Three

Memory is not
a test of truth;
just because man
fails to remember
his past lives
does not prove
he never had them.

Chapter Thirty-Eight
Page Three Hundred Forty-Seven

Unlike the spacial,
three-dimensional
physical world
cognized only by
the five senses,
the astral spheres
are visible to the
all-inclusive sixth sense—
intuition.

Chapter Forty-Three
Page Four Hundred Four

Man depends upon solids,
liquids, gases, and energy
for sustenance;
astral beings
sustain themselves
principally
by cosmic light.

Chapter Forty-Three
Page Four Hundred Five

The soul
expanded into Spirit
remains alone
in the region
of lightless light,
darkless dark,
thoughtless thought,
intoxicated with its ecstasy
of joy in God's dream
of cosmic creation.

Chapter Forty-Three
Page Four Hundred Eleven

Saints like Gandhi
have made not only
tangible material sacrifices,
but also the more
difficult renunciation
of selfish motive
and private goal,
merging their inmost being
in the stream of
humanity as a whole.

Chapter Forty-Four
Page Four Hundred Twenty-Five

It hath been said
that the continuation
of species is due to
man's being forgiving.
Forgiveness is holiness,
by forgiveness the universe
is held together.

Chapter Forty-Four
Page Four Hundred Thirty One

Misery, starvation,
and disease are
whips of our karma
which ultimately
drive us
to seek the true
meaning of life.

Chapter Forty-Six
Page Four Hundred Fifty-Three

A Selection of
Other Crystal Clarity Books

Moments of Truth —Volume One

Exerpts from *The Rubaiyat of Omar Khayyam Explained* by Paramhansa Yogananda, edited by J. Donald Walters. Here are some of the most insightful thoughts from *The Rubaiyat of Omar Khayyam Explained* (a commentary on the classic poem) placed in a thought-a-page layout that allows reflection on the simplicity, depth and practicality of each saying. Each illustrated excerpt is a refreshing, uplifting, immediately helpful thought. A must for anyone seeking inspiration and self-discovery.

Autobiography of a Yogi by Paramhansa Yogananda.

The original 1946 edition of the classic spiritual autobiography, which relates the life of Yogananda, the first yoga master of India whose mission it was to live and teach in the West. This book has helped launch, and continues to inspire, a spiritual awakening throughout the Western world.

The Rubaiyat of Omar Khayyam Explained by Paramhansa Yogananda. Nearly 50 years ago Yogananda discovered a scripture previously unknown to the world. It was hidden in the beautiful, sensual imagery of the beloved poem, *The Rubaiyat of Omar Khayyam*. His commentary reveals the spiritual mystery behind this world-famous love poem. Long considered as a celebration of earthly pleasure, now The Rubaiyat is revealed to be a profound spiritual teaching.

The Essence of Self-Realization compiled by J. Donald Walters. A remarkable collection of never-before-published quotations by Paramhansa Yogananda. It offers as complete an explanation of life's true purpose, and of the way to achieve that purpose, as may be found anywhere.

The Path: One Man's Quest on the Only Path There Is by J. Donald Walters (Swami Kriyananda). The moving story of Mr. Walters' search for meaning, and it's fulfillment during his years of training under Paramhansa Yogananda. In over 400 stories and sayings of Yogananda, the reader is given an inspiring glimpse into what it was like to live with one of the great masters of modern times.

Meditation for Starters by J. Donald Walters. This book gives both beginning and long-time meditators proven techniques and powerful visualizations for achieving inner peace. Written with simplicity and clarity, it also provides a way for readers to look at meditation as a "starting point" for everything they do. The companion audio is available separately on both CD and cassette, or can be purchased as a set with the book.

Ananda Yoga for Higher Awareness. A unique approach by J. Donald Walters, teaching hath yoga as it was originally intended—as a way to uplift consciousness and aid spiritual development. Illustrated with photos, it includes suggested routines for all levels, lays flat for easy reference, and offers powerful affirmations to help deepen the mind/body effect.

Rays of the Same Light. Parallel passages from the Bible and Bhagavad Gita, with commentary by J. Donald Walters. Rays probes the underlying similarities between these two great scriptures, and presents deep mystical teaching blended with practical common sense.

The "Secrets" Series by J. Donald Walters.
A thought for each day of the month.

Secrets of Love
Secrets of Happiness
Secrets of Friendship
Secrets of Inner Peace
Secrets of Meditation
Secrets of Success
Secrets of Self-Acceptance
Secrets for Women
Secrets for Men
Secrets of Prosperity
Secrets of Leadership
Secrets of Radiant Health and Well-being
Secrets of Emotional Healing
Secrets of Bringing Peace on Earth

(for children)
Life's Little Secrets
Little Secrets of Happiness
Little Secrets of Friendship
Little Secrets of Success

For information about these or other
Crystal Clarity products call: **1-800-424-1055**

A Selection of Music From
Clarity Sound & Light

I, Omar—J. Donald Walters—If the soul could sing, here would be its voice. I, Omar is inspired by The Rubaiyat of Omar Khayyam. Its beautiful melody is taken up in turn by English horn, oboe, flute, harp, guitar, cello, violin, and strings. The reflective quality of this instrumental album makes it a perfect companion for quiet reading or other inward activities.

Mantra—Kriyananda (J. Donald Walters)—For millennia, the Gayatri Mantra and the Mahamrityunjaya Mantra have echoed down the banks of the holy river Ganges. Allow the beauty of these sacred sounds to penetrate every atom of your being, gently lifting you to a state of pure awareness. Chanted by J. Donald Walters to a rich tamboura accompaniment.

AUM, Mantra of Eternity—the healing sound of the eternal mantra AUM, sung repeatedly to a rich tamboura accompaniment. The soothing voice of Kriyananda, direct disciple of Paramhansa Yogananda, on one continuous track. Powerful and inspiring!

Himalayan Nights—Agni/Howard—Seamless sitar, tabla, and tamboura on one continuous track—a soothing tapestry of sound. Use Himalayan Nights as a relaxing musical background for any daily activity.

CRYSTAL CLARITY
A new concept in living

Crystal Clarity means to see oneself, and all things as aspects of a greater reality; to seek to enter into conscious attunement with that reality and to see all things as channels for the expression of that reality.

It means to see truth in simplicity; to seek always to be guided by the simple truth, not by opinion; and by what is, not by one's own desires or prejudices.

It means striving to see things in relation to their broadest potential.

In one's association with other people it means seeking always to include their realities in one's own.